Digital

Storytelling

In and Out of the Classroom

Kay Teehan

A Professional Development Resource

To Larry,

my husband and my best friend.

ISBN: 978-1-4303-0092-2

Table of Contents

Chapter Four: Digital Storytelling Resources

Chapter Five: Planning for Digital Storytelling

Chapter Six: Implementing Digital Storytelling Lessons

Chapter Eleven: Putting it All Together

About the Author

Kay Teehan is a career educator and Media Specialist in Florida. She has a BA in Education and MS in Educational Technology. She received certification from the National Board for Professional Teaching Standards in 2002 in the area of Library/Media. She is presently a member of the Advisory Board for Channel One News, a nationally broadcasted daily current events and news program directed at secondary students. She is one of 30 Florida Master Digital Educators who work with the Florida Center for Instructional Technology in conjunction with the Florida Department of Education and University of South Florida to deliver cutting-edge technology skills instruction to educators all over the state of Florida.

Besides facilitating instruction in technology, Kay also is involved in the Alternative Certification Education program that trains individuals who enter educational careers without the necessary preparation to receive full teacher certification. She is a curriculum developer for both technology and ACE areas.

Kay has presented at state and national conventions on various technology topics including presentations at: Florida Educational Technology Conference, National Middle School Association Conference, Florida Association for Media Education Conference, National School Board Association Conference, and the National Conference for National Board Certified Teachers.

Introduction

Digital Storytelling is a tool that was created to integrate the newest technology in the classroom. It has proven to be a powerful tool indeed. I believe the reason for its power lies with the type of students we teach each day in our schools. Students today are multi-taskers, creative, and visual learners. They have grown up in a world of multimedia and respond to audio-visual in positive ways. Given the opportunity to tell their stories using digital storytelling models, they are transformed into self-motivated information consumers. Our job, as educators, becomes one of utilizing their natural gravitation to technology to fit our purposes of teaching state and national standards.

This book is not intended to be a "how-to" manual of creation of digital stories, although I have included information of where to find this information. This book, rather, is a manual of tips and resources on how to integrate the digital storytelling tool into your curriculum. The true influence of this educational tool is in the application of its appeal to our students in teaching and learning important curriculum standards in an exciting and motivating fashion. In this book, you will find the resources and help you need to make your classroom come alive with the use of digital assignments.

Although Digital Storytelling is a classroom tool, I have found that its application reaches far beyond the school door. Because the resources and software are available on home computers, digital storytelling has functioned as a scrapbooking tool to archive family events using an audio-visual format. I have included a few chapters to help you use this tool to document your personal life and the lives of those close to you. I have heard that digital storytelling may be the next great hobby of the world. If that is true, you will want to learn these skills to not only record your personal events, but also to pass on these skills to others.

Finally, this book is a personal compilation of what I know about Digital Storytelling from experience and from the belief that this tool will be the fastest growing application instrument for teachers to use as authentic assessment of student learning. I see this technology as a beginning of a new technique of student expression of learning and sharing what they have learning with others. Once teachers have tried this method of teaching research and information skills, they will find it so attractive that they will want to find more and more possible ways to use it. When that happens, I hope you will share your experiences with me and other educators. Sharing what we know and do is what 21st century teaching is all about.

Digital Storytelling

IN the Classroom

Chapter 1

What is Digital Storytelling?

R ead me a story is a phrase familiar to any parent. Children love stories, and seemingly never tire from hearing them repeatedly. As parents, we use story time to not only spend quality time with our kids, but to also pick stories that teach them about making good decisions and the consequences faced by characters that make bad choices. Stories have been used by us and our ancestors to teach morals and values of our culture, whether we are consciously aware of this or not. In most homes, stories provide a tradition that is remembered and cherished forever. As we move into the digital age, so have our stories in the form of movies, television, and recorded messages. Now, the art of storytelling is also making the leap into the world of technology.

Digital Storytelling is – at it's heart – telling stories in the tradition of countless generations before us – and using cutting-edge technology to do so. It has evolved from the earliest cave paintings, where man tried to explain his surrounding physical world and his need to communicate his experience with other humans. Storytelling grew into a method of recording the actions or qualities of one's ancestors, in the hopes that this would provide some sort of immorality. (Pellowski, 1977)

There are records of storytelling from every culture, and in many languages. Early history tells of Bards who combined storytelling with music and poetry to entertain and enlighten their audience. Epic tales such as Homer's "Iliad" grew out of the bard tradition and extended through such classic tales as "Merry Adventures of Robin Hood" and India's great tale "The Ramayana". Men such as the Brothers Grimm and Hans Christian Anderson began to collect the stories which common people told each other and storytelling began to be used to teach children proper behaviors and morals.

Various religious figures such as Jesus and Buddha told stories, or parables, to teach important positions of their beliefs. This method of teaching our children about religion is still the primary teaching tool today.

Benefits of Storytelling

No matter what the purpose of telling stories or what method we use to tell the story, there are certain benefits that are provided by using storytelling to communicate ideas. In their research, John Brown, Steve Denning, Katalina Groh and Larry Prusak list these potential benefits:

Communicate collaboratively: In abstract discussions, ideas come at us like missiles, invading our space and directing us to adopt a mental framework established by another being, and our options boil down to accepting or rejecting it, with all the baggage of yes-no winner-loser confrontations. Narrative by contrast comes at us collaboratively inviting us gently to follow the story arm-in-arm with the listener. It is more like a dance than a battle.

Communicate persuasively: When the listener follows a story, there is the possibility of getting the listener to invent a parallel story in the listener's own environment. Since we all love our own babies, the story so co-created becomes our own, and something we love and are prepared to fight for.

Communicate accurately: Before the advent of instant global communications, there was less awareness of the context in which knowledge arises. When communications were among people from the same village, or district, or city, one could often assume that the context was the same. With global communications, the assumption of similar context becomes obviously and frequently just plain wrong. Storytelling provides the context in which knowledge arises, and hence becomes the normal vehicle for accurate knowledge transfer.

Communicate intuitively: We know more than we realize. The role of tacit knowledge has become a major preoccupation because it is often the tacit knowledge that is most valuable. Yet if we do not know it, how can we communicate it? Storytelling provides an answer since by telling a story with feeling; we are able to communicate more than we explicitly know. Our body takes over and does it for us, without consciousness. Thus although we know more than we can tell, we can, through storytelling, tell more than we (explicitly) know.

Communicate entertainingly: Abstract communications are dull and dry because they are not populated with people but with things. As living beings we are attracted to what is living, and repelled by inert things such as concepts. Stories enliven and entertain.

Communicate movingly to get action: Storytelling does not just close the knowing-doing gap. It eliminates the gap by stimulating the listener to co-create the idea. In the process of co-creation, the listener starts the process of implementation in such a way that there is no gap.

Communicate feelingly: For all the talk about emotional intelligence, explicit talk about feelings can be cloying. Storytelling enables discussion of emotions in culturally acceptable and elegant way.
Communicate interactively: Unlike abstract talk, storytelling is inherently interactive. The storyteller sparks the story that the listeners co-create in their own minds. (Brown, Denning, Groh, & Prusak, 2004)

Therefore, for the earliest storytellers who told tales around campfires to try to explain the mysteries of the world around them, it was a way to mass information for understanding. Even though we now have come to understand many of the frightening mysteries which frustrated early man, our world is still in many ways a turbulent and unpredictable place, and we are still engaged in the ancient art of storytelling to try to build bridges of understanding in our world. We no longer sit around campfires, but employ the latest technological tools we have developed to tell our stories. We go to see movies, watch television shows, and rent videos from Blockbuster - all in our attempt to be entertained, informed, influenced, and taught through storytelling. Even the commercials we watch on television everyday are actually well crafted stories that have a beginning, middle, and an end – a message – and often a moral – all in 30 seconds.

Modern Storytelling

Have you checked you e-mail today? People utilize the Internet to communicate stories to the friends and colleagues (including the ever-popular Urban Myth) which they feel you cannot live without. With the universal use of PDA's, video phones, MP3 players, video cameras, computers & interactive software, we continue the tradition of storytelling in our everyday life. Thus, we have entered the arena of digital storytelling and some say with the tools most of us have readily available to us now, telling our stories in a digital manner will soon become the world's newest and most prevalent hobby. I have no doubt that this may occur—after all, it is a human invention that improves and an old tradition and we will continue to improve on in this generation and many more to come. Storytelling, it seems, is timeless.

Chapter 2

Digital Storytelling in the Classroom

I am a true advocate of using Digital Storytelling as a classroom tool. Many of us tell stories as a natural part of our teaching style, and have found it effective.

Storytelling involves many of the techniques of a well-planned lesson. It has a beginning, middle, end, and often an anticipatory set to help motivate attention. Great lesson plans are designed to inform, stimulate creative thinking, and entertain as well. Moving our stories into a digital format is the next generation of education and teaching our students to tell their own digital stories is its natural by-product. And since we already have access to the tools to utilize digital storytelling, all we require is: 1) to learn the skills to use the tools, and 2) the desire to teach lessons that use the media that most of our students are already using, and 3) the creativity to make learning more interesting, stimulating, and fun.

Benefits of the Educational Process

Digital Storytelling brings with it solid educational reasons for its use. There are many benefits for students and teachers in learning and teaching using this technology. Many of the new strategies teachers employ in the classroom are easily incorporated into Digital Storytelling lessons. When students create digital stories, they are involved in most or all of the following skills:

- Student becomes an active, participatory learner
- Student uses organization skills (CRISS strategies; BIG6 strategies)
- Student participates in an alternative learning style
- Student assesses information through authentic means
- Student performs authentic tasks (Life skills)
- Student participates in peer coaching activities
- Student collaborates on projects and works collegially (KAGEN strategies)
- Student uses higher-level thinking levels in evaluation, application, and synthesis of ideas
- Student achieves content achievement at an engagement level much higher than report writing and internalizes knowledge
- Student becomes a communicator of knowledge to others
- Student becomes a designer of effective and stimulating communication
- Student masters research skills and information seeking strategies
- Student utilizes inquiry-based learning
- Student participates in instructional change
- Student integrates technology into curriculum projects
- Student participates in peer review
- Student uses authentic project-based outcomes to share their work

- o Student utilizes reflection in a way which improves their skills
- o Student participates in planning, writing, and narrating projects which promotes reading literacy in its truest format

Meeting State and National Standards

Moreover, Digital Storytelling meets state and national educational standards on many different levels:

- First, it meets national computer and media literacy standards as put forth by Federal No Child Left Behind legislation and which the International Society for Technology in Education (ISTE) describes in its published National Educational Technology Standards (NETS). These standards can be found online at http://cnets.iste.org/. The standards ask that both students and teachers have the appropriate skills necessary to use hardware, software applications, media tools, and other forms of electronic technology. These tools are used in digital storytelling to produce and facilitate communication of information.

- Second, it meets Information Literacy standards found in most state educational standards. As a Media Specialist, I often collaborate with classroom teachers on ways to meet these reading & research standards. They call for student acquisition, interpretation, and dissemination of information. They focus on skills needed to locate, evaluate, use, and generate information. With the use of the Internet, these skills also encompass technology-based information and the strategies for finding primary and secondary sources that are now available for students. In digital storytelling, students must research information needed to assure accuracy in their finished project.

- Third, it meets the standards and demands of abilities needed to succeed in today's (and tomorrow's) technological world. This is where students make use of learned content material and manipulate it using technology tools. It combines knowledge with devices and skills - and that combination can be used to communicate, solve problems, and springboard to new ideas. The use of digital storytelling can be a useful life skill primarily because it can speak to people's inner souls and engage them in content areas they may not be otherwise interested. Well-developed digital stories use technology to elicit basic emotional responses to the subject matter. This taps into the creativity of students in an arena they have a natural affinity—the arena of technology.

Digital Storytelling and Higher-Level Thinking Skills

There is a tremendous difference in the end-products of assigning a typical topical research project to students, as compared to assigning a research project where critical questions lead students into digital storytelling. In the typical project, students rarely venture from the lower levels of Bloom's Taxonomy – those of Knowledge, Comprehension, and maybe even Application. The following chart will demonstrate the procedure involved when a student is assigned a typical research:

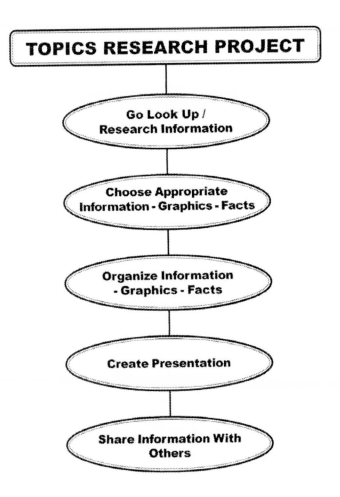

TOPICS RESEARCH PROJECT

Go Look Up /
Research Information

Choose Appropriate
Information - Graphics - Facts

Organize Information
- Graphics - Facts

Create Presentation

Share Information With
Others

In this graphic display, the student is assigned a topic – i.e.
" Research the culture of China today and present your findings in a
multimedia report to the class in order to share your information."

Most teachers then introduce the various methods available for
authentic technology presentation (PowerPoint, Keynote, iMovie,
MovieMaker, etc – see Chapter 3 for detail on the media tools). They
teach how to interact with these application software programs-and
most students respond positively to this task. Most traditional
assignments will use these programs to give reports. Another tool that
has been in general use in recent years is the utilization of one of the
Research Models (BIG6, Super3, FINDS, FACTS, etc.). These models

approach the task of student research from different perspectives; however, they all have, as their primary goal, to create organization for student research and allow intervention of "just-in-time" teacher direction into the process. These models have proven effective in creating a systematic process for students to research, organize data, and create reports. And, there is no doubt that the models have an important place in any research assignment; however, they do not address the quality of information that is sought, found, recorded, and ultimately reported in the multimedia report.

The student looks for information about China's culture using pre-taught online search strategies and library skills for print reference. They read and take notes on all information, graphics, and facts that have to do with the culture in China. They note proper citations for where they found the material. They take their notes, graphics, and facts and arrange and organize them in to some sort of order -putting together information on religion in one pile, customs in another pile, food preferences in another, etc. They then transfer the knowledge, facts, and graphics they have compiled into a multimedia report that at best summarizes, describes, and defines the culture of China. They have completed the requirements of the assignment without having to really think about the information beyond spelling the words correctly. They have not interacted with the information that would require them to analyze, evaluate, and synthesize the information - all of the higher level thinking skills. By the time the reach the last step of the assignment - that of sharing the information with the class – they are mere reporters of the information and have not truly engaged with the material at a deeper level. Because of this, they have not internalized or assimilated the concepts involved in China's culture, and can not possible apply the information to new circumstances outside of the report itself.

In the next graphic display, let us look at the differences that occur when the student is assigned to do a digital story:

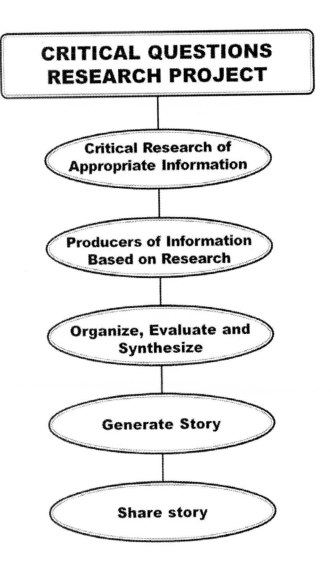

CRITICAL QUESTIONS RESEARCH PROJECT

- Critical Research of Appropriate Information
- Producers of Information Based on Research
- Organize, Evaluate and Synthesize
- Generate Story
- Share story

Here we see a difference beginning in the planning process of the assignment. Teachers using digital stories as the outcome project do not assign topical assignments—but rather critical questions which will lead students to research content areas with a different purpose in mind – that of telling a story. For instance, instead of assigning research on the culture of China, one would make this assignment: "Create a digital story about what it is like to be a woman in China today".

The same instruction of methods of reporting information must be addressed and the same use of research models such as BIG6 applies to this model; however, when the student begins researching the material, they do so with a much different purpose:

- They must critically evaluate the facts and information they find.

- They internalize what they read and take notes on the facts and data that will be included in their story.

- They seriously evaluate the graphics they collect because they need specific visuals to give their story impact.

- They take on the role as a producer of information based on their research that often gives us glimpses of their opinions about the information they are reporting.

- They cite their sources, but instead of noting bland facts and data, they will most likely make notes on the material that incorporate their own feelings.

- They actually begin to synthesize the material as they collect it.

When they begin to generate their digital story, they do it with still another purpose in mind. Students know from a lifetime of listening to stories, that good stories captivate the audience and they want to create a story that will do just that. They will want to design a multimedia presentation that not only informs, but entertains as well. They engage with the material on a much deeper level, evaluating, self-assessing, and redesigning as they proceed. They want to produce a product in which they have invested personal emotions, and they assimilate the information in the creation of the story. By the time they reach the final step – sharing their story – they have not only learned about China's culture, they have formed opinions about it, and will want to share their thoughts with others using state-of-the-art technology. It touches their very soul. They have not only learned the content material assigned, they have learned "how-to-think" about the material also.

Students also learn life skills of using convincing communication to inform, report, and enlighten others. They learn how to use technology tools to serve their own personal purposes. They learn how to form opinions and communicate their ideas. They learn the objectives of the lesson – China's culture – but the other lessons learned are perhaps just as important.

To view an excellent example of what a digital story that was student produced to answer the essential question: "What would it be like to be a woman in China today?", watch this online digital movie produced by four students at Brooks Magnet School in Wichita, Kansas entitled "Grass Born to be Stepped On":

http://www.digitales.us/story_details.php?story_id=12

Research & Literacy Skills

The four students who produced this digital story participated in almost the exact areas of research—culture, religion, demographics, geography, etc. – as the students researching using the traditional topic assignment format; however, these students approached the research with a purpose much more evaluative in nature. They were researching aspects of China to find out what exactly are the rights of women living there today, have those rights changed in recent years, and what impact it makes on Chinese women's daily lives. Moreover, they researched these topics with the ultimate goal of telling their findings in story format using digital technology to share what they learn with others. In watching the digital story, the viewer gets a sense of the deep resentment these young girls feel for how their counterparts in China live. Many times, growing up in a democratic society such as America, our children do not fully realize how their country provides them freedoms that do not exist in other parts of the world. Their teacher had to find it to be a satisfying experience to watch these students discover this knowledge, analyze it against their own lives, and tell their story in such a powerful and dramatic way. It is this higher-level learning and thinking that all teachers strive to instill in their students, and using digital storytelling to share their ideas and opinions is an optimal use of technology in the classroom.

It is plain to see that using digital storytelling is a major improvement of the process of researching and reporting information. And, it is the seamless integration of technology into the curriculum that demonstrates the best possible use of today's digital tools.

Types of Digital Stories

In "Grass Born to be Stepped On", we have just seen an example of a digital story as a vehicle for student research reporting. However, there are many other uses that can be assigned to digital storytelling. Here is a partial list:

- o Student created short stories
- o Retelling of folk tales or myths
- o Student created poetry
- o Book reports
- o Biographies
- o Persuasive narratives
- o Advertisements
- o Oral histories
- o History Fair projects
- o How-to-do-it directions

Students themselves will find uses across the curriculum to tell their stories. The integration of technology into all subject areas can be readily accomplished through the utilization of digital stories. Moreover, despite the growing pains you may encounter in teaching students to create digital stories, you will be more than satisfied with the results of your efforts.

In the next chapter, we will look at steps on how this integration process of digital technology can be incorporated into lesson plans in all curriculum areas.

Chapter 3

Technology Tools for Digital Storytelling

Y ou will need both hardware and software tools to facilitate the creation of digital stories in the classroom. However, there are so many options you can choose from to accommodate storytelling, and you probably already have everything you need available to you. In this chapter, you will see a variety of tools from which you can pick the level of sophistication your students can attain in telling their stories.

Hardware

The first necessary component is, of course, the computer. It does not matter much if you work in a PC or MAC platform environment, because there is great software available for both. MAC, of course, has magnificent graphic capabilities, but for student projects, PC platforms are just as easy and the results can be just as stunning. Because so many resources are available on the Internet, other hardware that is used in the process are optional, but nice to have and will make your students' stories more personal. These tools include a scanner, a digital camera, a video recorder, and a CD or DVD burner.

Because digital storytelling involves many class periods, one tool that I have found essential in a flash drive (or thumb drive) for each student group who are collaborating on a story. I have found that the 1 GB flash drives will hold all the graphics, articles, and video that my Middle School students research online, as well as their completed story. In High School, where the research and digital stories may be more complicated and lengthy, a 2GB flash drive should be plenty. This method of storing data during the development process assures that whether students work on the project in the school computer lab, in the Media Center, at the public library, or at home, they will have a convenient and safe way of securing their ongoing work. If you have the luxury of having ample computer access in your classroom to accommodate your students, this might be another optional tool for you. However, if you are like most of us in schools today, our students have to grab computer time here and there and everywhere and the flash drive becomes essential.

Another tool I find is optional in some cases, but essential for most, is the headset/microphone combination. I want my students to create stories that have audio – either music or narration – and the headset/microphone accommodates this process without the noise in the classroom and/or computer lab that occurs with speakers. Most of these headset/microphone combos are reasonably priced now and even the lowest priced combos have good quality and are sufficient for student use. This tool becomes essential when the student narrates the story, as other computer microphones tend to pick up too much ambient noise.

Software

You can build a digital story using PowerPoint, Keynote, Kidspix, Hyperstudio, Kidspiration or Inspiration. The main components of telling a story can be adapted to the restrictions of each of these programs, and some of these methods allow for audio as well as video storytelling. However, other software that is readily available will really get your student's creativity levels to soar. (NOTE: I realize that many web pages are frequently edited or changed or renamed. The websites listed here are current as of this printing, however, if you have trouble with any of them try truncating to the home page site and search for the link needed.)

- ○ <u>Apple iMovie and Windows MovieMaker 2</u>

Whether you use PC or MAC, these options of software applications are easy to teach to students. Both programs allow for combining images with video clips, music, audio narration, and super effects for zooming, panning, and editing graphics (what I describe as the Spielberg effect to my students). They also have abundant transitions that make the movie flow seamlessly as well as the addition of titles and credits. Both programs come with your favorite platform and both are drag-and-drop easy to use. Both programs have systematic tutorials available at the individual websites. Both will add pizzazz to student projects.

- ○ <u>Audacity (MAC and Windows)</u>

Audacity is an editing tool that is easy to use in both platforms. It allows the student to record a narration audio track, edit it, import WAV, AIFF, AU and MP files for use in their stories. They can even create multi-track recordings by dubbing over existing tracks or add special effects to audio files such as echos, phasers, or wahwahs. Audacity is a free, open source program available for download at: http://audacity.sourceforge.net/

You will find other uses for Audacity besides storytelling as it can also be used to convert tapes and records into digital recordings and or to splice sounds together. Other uses can be found at the website.

o   PhotoStory3 (Windows)

PhotoStory3 is available for users of Windows XP at the
Microsoft site free of charge.   Although its video is limited to the use
of still images, it provides for addition of soundtracks and voice
narrations, and has most of the cool effects and features found on
MovieMaker that allow for cropping, rotating, and other editing of
images. Tutorials of how to use this drag-and-drop program as well as
the download of the program can be found at:
http://www.microsoft.com/windowsxp/using/digitalphotography/photost
ory/default.mspx . This is a great place for beginning storytellers to get
started.

o   Comic Life (MAC) and Comic Book
    Creator(Windows)

Both of these programs cost less than $30 to purchase, but have
excellent classroom uses. Comic Life, by Freeverse, allows the student
to drop digital images into their choice of comic book format templates,
crop and edit the images, then add speech balloons, captions and special
effects lettering to enable them to tell their story. There are many
ways to save the finished product, including TIFF, GIF, JPEG, PNG,
HTML, iPhoto and Quicktime. The cost is $29.95 and can be downloaded
at: http://www.freeverse.com/comiclife/ . Comic Book Creator, by
Planetwide Games, is the Windows version of Comic Life and has
incorporated most of its effects. It adds the capability of capturing
screenshots from your favorite video games to incorporate into your
story and allows the finished product to be saved as a PDF file. The cost
is $29.99 and an upgrade product (also $29.99) called BOOM! will allow
your comic strips to add animation. Comic Book Creator has a wonderful
online tutorial for its product and can be downloaded at:
http://www.mycomicbookcreator.com/frontpage.php

o   Bubbleshare

This tool is a very easy tool for students to use.   It is also a
place where students can share their stories online. You will need to
register for a free account and create an album for your students
(student work needs to be private and not available to the public and this
feature is accommodated in this program). Students can upload photos
and add sounds, titles, and bubble captions to their work.   The results

are great. You can find out more about this product at: http://www.bubbleshare.com/

    o   CrazyTalk4 (by Reallusion)

This is facial animation & lip-sync software that uses facial animated morphing techniques to bring any digital image to life. You can record or import audio and combine it with animated expressions and even some emotions to bring a still picture to life using head movement, shoulder movement, eye movement, and lip shapes.   Imagine having the Statue of Liberty narrate a digital movie on Immigration, or even your favorite pet narrating your collection of Holiday photos. Finished products can be saved in many formats for inclusion in other projects as well. This product cost $49.95 and can be downloaded at: http://www.reallusion.com/default.asp

    o   Adobe Photoshop Elements 4.0

This software will edit and enhance your photos by fixing common flaws instantly or using advanced options for more control. This product costs around $90 and can be downloaded at: http://www.adobe.com/products/photoshopelwin/

    o   Adobe Premiere Elements 2.0

After you master MovieMaker2 or iMovie, you may want to upgrade your skills with this software. This software comes with even more special effects and the addition of Digital Dolby sound. It sells for around $100 and a 30-day free trial download can be found at: http://www.adobe.com/products/premiereel/

Tutorials for using Digital Storytelling Software

Windows MovieMaker Download:

http://www.microsoft.com/windowsxp/downloads/updates/moviemaker2.mspx

Windows MovieMaker Tutorials:

http://www.microsoft.com/windowsxp/using/moviemaker/default.mspx

http://www.microsoft.com/windowsxp/using/moviemaker/getstarted/default.mspx

http://www.mightycoach.com/articles/mm2/index.html

http://www.mightycoach.com/articles/mm2/savingprojects-moviemaker2.html

http://www.ita.sel.sony.com/support/tutorials/usb-streaming/

http://www.fluffbucket.com/othettutorials/video/wmmaker.htm

http://www.atomiclearning.com/moviemaker2

http://www.windowsmoviemakers.net/Tutorials/HowToMovieMaker.aspx

http://core.ecu.edu/vel/itc/tutorials/moviemaker.html

http://www.eicsoftware.com/PapaJohn/MM2/PS3-Intro.html

http://www.bobsedulinks.com/digital.htm

Microsoft PhotoStory Download:

http://www.microsoft.com/windowsxp/using/digitalphotography/photostory/default.mspx

Microsoft PhotoStory Tutorials:

http://www.eicsoftware.com/PapaJohn/MM2/PS3-Intro.html

http://www.eicsoftware.com/PapaJohn/MM2/MM2.html

http://www.bobsedulinks.com/digital.htm

http://www.microsoft.com/windowsxp/using/digitalphotography/photostory/tips/create.mspx

http://msmvps.com/chrisl/archive/2004/10/27/16816.aspx

http://www.windowsphotostory.com/

http://graphicssoft.about.com/b/a/122245.htm

Windows Media Player 10 Download:

http://www.microsoft.com/downloads/details.aspx?FamilyID=b446ae53-3759-40cf-80d5-cde4bbe07999&displaylang=en

Other Tools

Other tools needed to do a successful digital storytelling project include Internet/Research tools, books, videos clips, audio clips, images and photographs, and, in some cases, access to experts in various subject areas. These resources will be covered in the next chapter.

Chapter 4

Digital Storytelling Resources

_____

The first requirement of creating good digital stories is to have good resources available to you to select quality photos, video, audio clips, music **and** the resources that allow you to format your story to include the technical features that allow you to invent creative ways to tell your story. In this chapter, you will find the resources I have found to be useful. Most are free to download, but a few are available for purchase and are worth every penny I paid for them.

Digital Video

Unitedstreaming Video ($)

I hate to begin with one of those resources that is not free; however, this one is so important for the classroom teacher that it deserves first mention. Unitedstreaming video is a collection of over 40,000 digital video clips, images, music, speeches & other audio clips, and text that are organized for easy access and searchable by subject and title. Most of the clips are editable and can be easily downloaded for use in your projects. Although there is a 30-day trail version available, you must own a subscription to this service to use them in your digital stories, and you must cite Unitedstreaming as your source. Because Unitedstreaming is owned by Discovery Education, you can be assured that the videos available are of the highest quality, screened for accuracy, and are even matched to most state standards. This product is a "must have" for all educators.
http://www.unitedstreaming.com

COSMEO ($)

Cosmeo is the unique homework help tool brought to you by Discovery Channel. It is designed to help students master challenging concepts. It is a subscription site ($9.95) but it includes:

- 30,00 video clips
- 20,000 images
- 27,000 text articles.

This resource is invaluable for students who are serious about digital storytelling. There is a 30-day free trail available.

The History Channel (FREE)

The History Channel offers some digital video clips and audio clips including great speeches of our times available for educational use and inclusion in digital stories. The selection frequently changes so check the site often for exciting choices you can use.

http://www.historychannel.com/broadband/home/

NASA's HubbleScope (FREE)

Some exciting video and images that are products of the Hubble Telescope are available for download from this site. Check out the incredible Black Hole video for breathtaking splendor. Also available at this site are still images and illustrations created by NASA to help explore our universe.

http://hubblesource.stsci.edu/sources/video/clips/

Edutopia (FREE)

The George Lucas Foundation, which sponsors Edutopia, has developed great videos on the topic of integrating video in classroom curriculum. These clips are good resources for telling stories about our journey into educational technology.

http://www.edutopia.org/video/frame.php

NOVAteachers (FREE)

PBS has created an online source for teachers to download portions of their NOVA Science series for classroom use. The clips are from 2-15 minutes in length. The subject matter covers the whole spectrum of Science & Math topics.

http://www.pbs.org/wgbh/nova/teachers/video.html

Frog Calls (FREE)

Sponsored by the Chicago Herpetological Society, this site offers digital video of toads and frogs as a tribute to the several species of amphibians that have gone extinct in the last few decades.
http://www.midwestfrogs.com/

Pfizer (FREE)

Pfizer Pharmaceuticals has an interesting site with free video clip downloads on the cell interaction in the development of the Aspergillus fungus that is thought to be responsible for the "sick building syndrome" in many places throughout the country. Anyway, the video clips are cool and can be inserted into digital stories.
http://www.aspergillus.org.uk/indexhome.htm?education/videoclips.htm~main

Center for Disease Control (FREE)

Almost 7000 video clips on health are available for download at this site.
http://www.cdc.gov/search.do?action=search&queryText=video

Rutgers Mosquito Resources (FREE)

This site has video clips on mosquito development and behavior.
http://www.rci.rutgers.edu/~insects/mosvid.htm

Splashes from the River (FREE)

This site contains videos on grammar and its importance in our society.

http://www.splashesfromtheriver.com/clips.htm

Earthballs (FREE)

Sponsored by Orbis, this is a very special site with spectacular video clips of Earth as viewed from outer space.

http://www.earthball.com/QTindex.html

Global Journeys (FREE)

Video clips that are student produced from trips taken by educational student travel.

http://www.global-journeys.com/Video%20Clips.htm

Poetic License (FREE)

The clips at this site show secondary students participating in a Poetry Slam event.

http://www.itvs.org/poeticlicense/film_clips.html

Humanities Extensions (FREE)

This is an extension program sponsored by North Carolina University. It shows video clips of everyday life in Asia, Africa, and the Pacific Rim.

http://www.ncsu.edu/chass/extension/video/

Internet Archive: Prelinger Collection (FREE)

This is a don't miss collection of advertising, educational, and industrial videos. It is a treasure house of vintage videos that you can use in digital storytelling.

http://www.archive.org/details/prelinger

Nature (FREE)

The Public Broadcasting Network has made video clips from its popular Nature Series available at this site.
http://www.pbs.org/wnet/nature/database.html

All the Web Search Engine: Videos (FREE)

Not all the clips you find here will be gems, but it is a source of a huge collection of video clips—but beware—not all will be educational.

http://www.alltheweb.com/?cat=vid&cs=utf8&q=&rys=0&itag=crv

Model Digital Stories

Digitales: The Art of Digital Storytelling

This is an amazing collection of both student produced and teacher produced digital stories. My personal favorites are:

- Grass Born to be Stepped On (student produced)
- My Father's Eyes: A Daughter's Prospective (teacher produced by my friend, Po Dickerson)

http://www.digitales.us/index.php

Center for Digital Storytelling

Click on the Resources tab for a collection of personal digital stories.

http://www.storycenter.org/whatis.html

Digital Stories from Niles Township High School

This collection of stories from high school students in Illinois are great examples for your students. My favorite is "Respectable Husband".

http://www.digitalstories.org/studentvideos.html

Tech Head Stories

At this site, you will find a variety of digital story types made with different media. My favorite –"Broken Sky".

http://tech-head.com/dstory.htm

Envision Your World

Click the "Timeline" to see an example of a digital story told in the format of a timeline.

http://www.envisionyourworld.com/welcome_edu.php

Next Exit

Dana & Denice Atchley created the "Digital Drive-In" to showcase digital stories.

http://www.nextexit.com/drivein/driveinframeset.html

Fray: Online Stories

A collection of digital stories using PowerPoint and Keynote media.

http://www.fray.com.is/mail/wonderscriber.cgi

Ken Burns: Telling a Story

The PBS site has examples of professional digital stories from the genius of Ken Burns.

http://www.pbs.org/civilwar/images/

Creative Narrations

Personal family digital stories. My favorite: "Troy's Story".

http://www.creativenarrations.net/site/storybook/index.html

Telling Their Stories: Oral History Archive Project

This site has video clips of interviews with Holocaust survivors, WWII camp liberators, and Japanese-American internees.

http://tellingstories.org/index.html

Audio Resources

Audacity

Audacity is free, open source software for recording and editing sounds. It can be downloaded free for both MAC and Windows platforms at:

http://audacity.sourceforge.net/

FreeAudioClips.com

FreeAudioClips.com is loaded with tons of wav, midi and au files for your listening and downloading pleasure!

http://www.freeaudioclips.com/

Free Audio Clips

There are several different types of audio files available in this library: **MIDI** (Musical Instrument Digital Interface) - Typically smallest in filesize; **AU** (Audio file) - The sound format for Java; **WAV** (Wave file) - The sound format for Windows.

http://resources.bravenet.com/audio_clips/

Bravenet

There are several different types of audio files available in this library: **MIDI** (Musical Instrument Digital Interface) - Typically smallest in file size; **AU** (Audio file) - The sound format for Java; **WAV** (Wave file) - The sound format for Windows.

http://resources.bravenet.com/audio_clips/

Garageband

This site is a great secret of MAC users everywhere. You can not only download music, but also create your own. Check it out!

http://www.garageband.com/htdb/index.html

Free Play Music

The Free Play Music Library is a comprehensive collection of High End Broadcast production music spanning all the popular musical genres, available for download either on-line or for purchase on CD.

http://www.freeplaymusic.com/

Image Resources

American Memories Collection

The United States Library of Congress has brought together more than 100 sets of images from different eras of American History. Thousands of photos have been digitized and made available online and are valuable tools for storytelling.

http://memory.loc.gov/ammem/index.html

Google Images

Don't discount the search engines for supplying good quality images for use in storytelling. Google is perhaps the most comprehensive image search engine today.

http://www.google.com

FreeImages

This site offers more than 2500 original stock photos online and free to use.

http://www.freeimages.co.uk/

Corbis

Beautiful photography that is royalty free for use and indexed by subject.

http://pro.corbis.com/

Ditto

Not only photo images but good clip art available here.

http://www.ditto.com/searchresults.aspx

Hubblesite

Some of the most beautiful and exotic photos from space are here and they are spectacular!

http://hubblesite.org/gallery/album/

Florida Center for Instructional Technology

This site, in cooperation with the University of South Florida, has collected amazing images of not only Florida, but also 3-D images, Holocaust images and Vietnam War images.

http://fcit.usf.edu/default.htm

Other Valuable Resources on Digital Storytelling

Digital Video in the Classroom

This site expounds on "*video production in the classroom enables the development of media literacy, higher order thinking skills, project based learning experiences, real world relevancy experiences, and a deeper connection to the curriculum being explored.*"

http://edtech.guhsd.net/video.html

Video Camera

This is the website for an Australian publication that covers all sorts of troubleshooting for problems involving camcorders.

http://www.videocamera.com.au/

Digital Video in Education

This website will offer some project ideas for K-12 classrooms, tutorials in the basics of digital video, some hints for getting started and some links to various resources.

http://www.mjsd1.ca/~rbl/dv/home.html

Dr, Jason Ohler

Jason Ohler offers excerpts on various presentations he has delivered on the power of digital computing in today's world.

http://www.jasonohler.com/presentations/video.cfm

Center for Intellectual Property

This site offers help in teaching students about copyright and plagiarism.

http://www.umuc.edu/distance/odell/cip/learningobjects.html

Video Production for Students

Kids' Vid is an instructional website to help teachers and students use digital video in project-based learning.

http://kidsvid.altec.org/

Teaching & Learning with Digital Video

This list provides links to selected resources on digital video in education. Quality of each resource was the main factor used in determining placement here.

http://www.kn.att.com/wired/fil/pages/listdvma.html

MovieMaker2 for Beginners

Need some pointers on using MovieMaker in your classroom?

http://www.microsoft.com/windowsxp/using/moviemaker/getstarted/default.mspx

Digital Music Files

Kathy Schrock shares information about using digital music files in the classroom.

http://school.discovery.com/schrockguide/newtheme0705.html

Ideas for Digital Storytelling across the Curriculum

Brainstorming list of ideas to "jump-start" your digital story lesson.

http://www.techteachers.com/digstory/ideas.htm

Rubric for Assessing Digital Stories

Charmaine Wierzbicki, from Indiana, shares a great rubric she uses with her 9th graders for assessing their digital stories.

http://www.discoveryeducatornetwork.com/objects/content_revision/download.cfm/revision_id.244324/workspace_id.124855/Digital%20Story%20Rubric.doc

Lesson Plan for Great Depression Digital Story Assignment

Gary Carmichael, a high school teacher from Montana, shares this great lesson plan.

http://www.discoveryeducatornetwork.com/objects/content_revision/download.cfm/revision_id.216439/workspace_id.124855/Great%20Depression%20Movie%20Assignment.doc/

Outline for Teaching MovieMaker2

Burt Lo, from California, shares this PowerPoint outline for teaching MovieMaker to your students.

http://www.discoveryeducatornetwork.com/objects/content_revision/download.cfm/revision_id.210698/workspace_id.124855/Outline%20for%20Teaching%20Movie%20Maker%202.pdf/

Using Digital Cameras in the Classroom

Jennifer Turney, a media specialist from Texas, has compiled a great list of the "how-to's" of using digital cameras with students.

http://www.discoveryeducatornetwork.com/objects/content_revision/download.cfm/revision_id.197344/workspace_id.124855/Using%20Digital%20Cameras%20and%20Pictures%20in%20the%20Classroom.doc/

Chapter 5

Planning for Digital Storytelling

Digital storytelling units begin with good planning, not unlike any good lesson you deliver to students. However, digital storytelling requires the teacher to plan for special areas in order to ensure a quality product. These areas included essential questions, organization, and application training.

The Essential Question

Essential questions set the stage for solid inquiry-based learning to take place. Sometimes called "guiding questions", they are worded in a way that require the student to use higher-level thinking strategies such as evaluation, problem-solving, analysis, and synthesizing of fact with opinion. The quality of the storytelling product largely depends on how the assignment is given; i.e. the use of well-written essential questions. Good essential questions must spark interest, motivate, and even intrigue the student. They serve to tie the content area objectives to real-life experience. They make the curriculum matter relevant to the student. Essential questions must make the student curious and ignite wonder. Answers to essential questions cannot be "looked up". They must be "invented". Good essential questions cross over rigid curriculum barriers to involve all content areas into providing input into the answers, i.e. using language arts and math skills to answer a science question.

The result of forming good essential questions is that they lead to a digital story that represents the authentic views of the student or group of students. In an age where education demands that we teach pre-set national and state standards, teachers know that one of the most important functions of school is not to "cover" the material, but to teach students to form opinions, beliefs, and attitudes about the material covered. In this way, students engage with the material in a real-world manner and sharing their outcomes with others using the technology of digital storytelling in a real-world skill. It becomes a "win-win" situation. State standards are taught, higher-level thought process is employed, and cutting-edge technology is utilized.

I believe that good essential question assignments are directly correlated with wonderful digital stories that are products of that assignment. Because of this, teachers need to plan well-crafted and well-worded essential questions. To do this, teachers need to look closely at the objectives they want to accomplish in the assignment, the standards they are required to meet, and quality of resources they have available for student use. It requires transforming objectives into essential questions. The following chart illustrates this transformation from objective to essential question:

Objective	Essential Question
5th grade: Student will give reasons for immigration to the United States during the 19th century.	Would you rather be an immigrant to the United States in 1890 or in 2006?

7th grade: Student knows the positive and negative consequences of human action on the Earth's systems.	As a television reporter in the year 2199, you are asked to do a documentary on the effects on the world due to global warming which will be called, "How did we Get Here?"
4th grade: Student will list the reasons for and outcomes of the Louisiana Purchase	How would America be different if the Louisiana Purchase never took place?
10th grade: Student will determine reasons for the Indian Wars during America's Westward Expansion and its relationship to the concept of Manifest Destiny.	Relate how the Indian/settler clashes during the Westward Expansion era in American history compare to the Israeli expansion of territory in recent years.
8th grade: Student will know that if more than one force acts on an object, then the forces can reinforce or cancel each other, depending on their direction and magnitude.	What would our world be like if you woke up tomorrow and the Magnetic forces on our planet were not functioning?

Given an intriguing essential question, the students can produce intriguing digital stories, how-to demonstrations, or advertisements, which use appropriate multi-media to communicate their ideas, opinions, and beliefs that are based on their research findings.

Organizing Students and the Process

The next part of the planning process is to set up a scheme to organize students in the process of research and production of their digital stories. Most students do not have the organizational skills necessary to complete a multi-task assignment such as digital storytelling. They may not know how to generate ideas (brainstorm) in a group setting. They need a method that enables them to integrate new and old knowledge, assess understanding of concepts, and assemble complex ideas into a structure that can be told using digital storytelling. They need aids to sequence their thoughts into a compelling story that has a beginning, middle, and end. Teaching students to do this is a skill they can use in many situations beyond research and storytelling, and there are many methods to help.

Student-produced concept maps will delineate what information they already know about a subject, what information they need to find, where they can look for the information they need, what order their information needs to be formatted in order to make sense. Although there are many formats available to use in organizing student research, my favorite is the BIG6 Information & Research model. Developed by educators Mike Eisenberg and Bob Berkowitz, BIG6 is probably the best-known and most used method for teaching researching and technology skills to students. The BIG6 strategy gets its name from the six steps in its model:

1. Task Definition

1.1   Define the information problem
1.2   Identify information needed

2. Information Seeking Strategies

2.1   Determine all possible sources
2.2   Select the best sources

3. Location and Access

3.1   Locate sources (intellectually and physically)
3.2   Find information within sources

4. Use of Information

4.1   Engage (e.g., read, hear, view, touch)
4.2   Extract relevant information

5. Synthesis

5.1   Organize from multiple sources
5.2   Present the information

6. Evaluation

6.1   Judge the product (effectiveness)

6.2   Judge the process (efficiency)

The model is based on the premise that all successful problem-solving strategies address all of the above steps – although not necessarily in linear order. It is based on the research of how humans find and process information and use information to solve problems. Some steps take very little time to complete, while other steps take days. I use the BIG6 as an anchor for my students to use during the digital storytelling assignment. The specific form I use with my Middle School students can be found at: http://www.sasaustin.org/library/assignmentOrganizer.php , but forms for younger students as well as more information about BIG6 can be found at: http://www.big6.com

Concept Mapping

Concept mapping using graphic organizers is also a good choice for getting students organized. Concept maps can be created using most word processing programs, but software that has been design specifically for student use is Inspiration (grades 6-12) or Kidspiration (grades K-5). If you have used this software before, you will see how it can be adapted to mapping out an organized approach to student research. If you have not used this software before, you can download a free 30-day trial at: http://www.inspiration.com/ .

Because it uses visual conceptualization as an organization tool, Inspiration and Kidspiration appeal to students who do not like to do pre-planning and outlining of assignments. The bonus is that once the concept map is complete, it can be turned into a traditional outline at the click of the mouse. On the following page, there is an example.

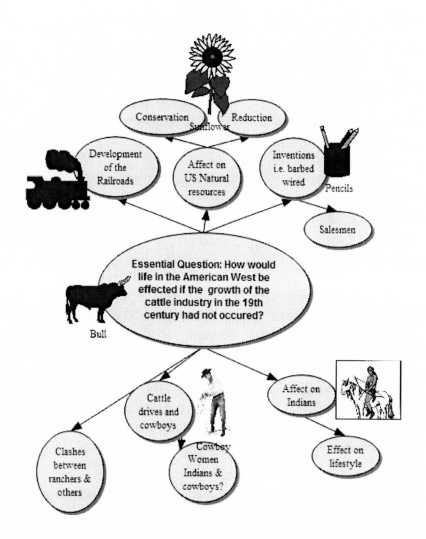

Conservation

Reduction

Sunflower

Development
of the
Railroads

Affect on
US Natural
resources

Inventions
i.e. barbed
wired

Pencils

Salesmen

**Essential Question: How would
life in the American West be
effected if the growth of the
cattle industry in the 19th
century had not occured?**

Bull

Cattle
drives and
cowboys

Affect on
Indians

Clashes
between
ranchers &
others

Cowboy
Women
Indians &
cowboys?

Effect on
lifestyle

With a click of the mouse, this previous diagram becomes the outline seen next:

Essential Question: How would life in the American West be effected if the growth of the cattle industry in the 19th century had not occurred?

    I.   Affect on US Natural resources

            A. Conservation

            B. Reduction

    II.   Affect on Indians

            A. Effect on lifestyle

    III.   Cattle drives and cowboys

            A. Women, Indians & Cowboys?

    IV   Development of the Railroads

    V.   Inventions i.e. barbed wired

            A. Salesmen

    VI.   Clashes between ranchers & others

Storyboarding

However, concept mapping is not the only organization that your students will need. After gathering all their information, they will need assistance in sequencing their story. The best way to accomplish this is with storyboards. There are many types of storyboards and I have listed sources of the ones I find most helpful, depending on which type of application I am using with my students to produce their digital story.

- http://www.open.ac.uk/crete/movingwords/pdf/storyboard.pdf

- http://www.stedwards.edu/pt3/DownloadDocs/Sample%20Storyboard%20Template.doc
- http://www.csupomona.edu/~wcweber/325/storybd.htm
- http://www.csd.org/showmemovie/storybrd.pdf
- http://www.glc.k12.ga.us/passwd/trc/ttools/attach/teachr/PowerPoint-Storyboard.doc
- http://www.glc.k12.ga.us/passwd/trc/ttools/attach/stu/ppstrybd.doc
- http://www.glc.k12.ga.us/trc/cluster.asp?mode=browse&intPathID=7801
- http://www.knowitall.org/bellsouthdigitalstoryteller/training/pdf/storyboard.pdf
- http://dmt.fh-joanneum.at/kd3/objects/application_pdf/video_storyboard_template_2screens_v10.pdf
- http://weblogs.elearning.ubc.ca/modernmedia/archives/V-A%20Storyboard%20Template.doc
- StoryBoard Pro (free software from Atomic Learning) & tutorial on how to create a storyboard: http://www.atomiclearning.com/storyboardpro
- Gliffy: http://www.gliffy.com/
- http://www.mediafestival.org/storyboard.pdf

There is built-in storyboarding help in both MovieMaker2 and iMovie applications, however I have found more success having students storyboard their scenes before going to the computer.

Teaching Production Skills

And speaking of computers, it brings us to the final part of the planning process – training students to use the application program you choose for the project. Students lucky enough to have access to a computer at home (or at Grandma's house, or the church, or the library, etc) are harboring the idea that they are computer literate. However, being successful in playing computer games or checking their e-mail or even writing a paper using a word processing program is not truly computer literacy. Often, schools lack the time, hardware, or software to teach the life-skills students will need in the real world. Sitting a student in front of a drill-and-kill program in the computer lab is not teaching them the abilities they need to operate the computer to its optimal potential. Computer literacy is not only "how" to use the computer, but also involves "when" and "why" to use the computer (Eisenberg & Johnson, 1996)

Therefore, teachers who embark on any inquiry-based unit that has as its outcome an authentic assessment project that requires computer application programs, need to plan for the extra time it will require teaching the application of the program itself. My experience has been that teaching these skills immediately before requiring their use in a project is much more successful than trying to teach the skills in isolation and unrelated to a classroom assignment. This integrated approach of tying computer skills directly to a curriculum area assignment takes much planning and may require your collaboration with Media Specialists, Technology Specialists, or other colleagues at your school site who can help you design and implement this lesson. Of course, the first step is that you become very acquainted with the programs, as you will be the ultimate troubleshooter of problems students may encounter along the way. You will soon learn, however, that the most successful digital storytelling lessons involve collaborative planning and implementation by teachers and Media Specialists. Do not be afraid to ask for their help to developing this unit because they are trained in information literacy skills that are necessary in today's digital world.

If you feel unqualified to teach programs such as PowerPoint, Keynote, iMovie, Inspiration, PhotoStory3, or MovieMaker2 to your students, you have a few options. If you cannot find a technology specialist to help you, there are several online tutorials that can help you and your students learn to utilize these (and other) powerful tools. Chapter 3 lists online tutorials you can use to become familiar with the various software.

One option is to buy a subscription to one of the web-based software training sites especially designed for schools. These sites offer short step-by-step videos that explain in detail how to use software programs. My favorite of this genre of tutorial sites is Atomic Learning and you can sign up for a 30-day free trial at: http://www.atomiclearning.com/home . Atomic Learning covers all the programs you want to use in creating digital stories for both Windows and MAC platforms. They also have great tutorials on using digital cameras and digital storytelling. Check it out!

If buying a subscription to one of these services is not possible because of lack of funding (and isn't that always the case!) then there are also some free online tutorials you can use with your students. Here are some of them:

- http://www.actden.com/
- http://www.internet4classrooms.com/on-line.htm
- http://www.educationonlineforcomputers.com/
- http://www.learningelectric.com/
- http://www.microsoft.com/education/tutorials.mspx

Learning the requisite skills to manipulate the software to tell a digital story is a vital part of a successful project. Students should be assessed on their use of the application program along with the content and mechanics of their story. In the chapter on assessing digital storytelling this will be made clearer, but you should know at the planning stage of your lesson that time needs to allowed for this process of learning how the software works. Think of it like this: Students will be learning software programs that will hold tremendous opportunity for future use both in work and personal situations, and they will be honing skills they need to thrive in our information-rich society.

Chapter 6

Implementing Digital Storytelling Lessons

I n this chapter, I intend to share with you the benefit of my experience. Working with students in research-based digital storytelling assignments, I have made mistakes and had many of those "I'll never do that again" moments that led to the invention of better ways to manage digital storytelling projects. This trial-and-error experience should not have to be repeated in schools all over again, so I will try to lead you away from the pitfalls.

The process is basic and can be revised or duplicated in every content area. This particular lesson outline is for a digital story produced using MovieMaker2:

1. Assign groups
2. Demonstrate & teach the software
3. Show exemplary digital stories
4. Assign task (essential questions)
5. Define expectations (rubric)
6. Begin research (concept mapping & research model)
7. Begin storyboarding
8. Write narration
9. Produce product
10. Publish and present production
11. Assess
12. Reflect

Let us look at each of these in detail.

1. Assign Groups

Unless you are working with older, sophisticated students, you will want to assign digital storytelling to small workgroups. The most successful stories I have seen have been a cooperative effort as a part of group structure. The students who work in the group are more engaged; more motivated, and have more fun. They usually do not want to disappoint their fellow students by not doing their best, and they actually learn from each other both information-seeking skills and technology skills. They are able to put their individual creativity in combination with that of others to add zest to the finished product. In addition, I have found that in groups, students interact with the content material on a deeper level and have enhanced retention of the subject matter. If you do not already work with students in cooperative learning groups, you may need to look at some of the research on teaching with interdependent workgroups. Group projects promote learning, enhance social skills, and are practice for real-life work that rarely involves strictly individual contribution.

That said, there are some guidelines you need to set down when using groups to perform tasks needed to produce a digital story.

- The group is going to sink or swim as a group. Each person needs to do his/her part to prevent sinking. There is no person in a group that is indispensable. Everyone's contribution is needed and expected. Roles & responsibilities of individual members should be discussed and assigned at the beginning of the project, and members of the group need to communicate if they are having a problem with their part of the assignment.
- Members of a group are expected to tutor each other on elements of the project in which they are proficient and others may be lacking. If no one in the group can figure out the answer, ask for help from the teacher immediately.
- Problems that arise between members of the group need to be brought to the attention of the teacher. We cannot waste time on petty arguments when so much is at stake in the assignment.

Take care in choosing which students will work on which team. You will want your group to be heterogeneous in almost every way – personality types, academic talent, technological talent, learning styles, etc. Once chosen, you need to monitor the groups to ensure that they are successfully working together and intervene when necessary.

2. Demonstrate & Teach Software

I have given you methods of teaching software applications to students in Chapter 5, however, I feel the need to reiterate the importance of the demonstration stage of this instruction to the learning of technology. I use an LCD projector and actually use pre-selected facts and graphics to create a digital story using MovieMaker2 on the screen for the class. I drag-and-drop images and video, create titles, create and insert narration and music, and insert effects and transitions. This modeling of a story is important to ease any fears that this is going to be too difficult for some students. They will clearly see that the process is easy and usually not time-consuming and they can relax and have fun with it.

3. Show Exemplary Digital Stories

Students need to see finished projects that exemplify the characteristics you want them to incorporate in their digital stories. In Chapter 4 there are online sites where you and choose student-produced digital stories that can serve as models. After viewing a digital story, discuss both the research requirements and technical requirements that were used in the creation of the story. After learning the individual software programs, they can then look at what that program produced in a typical assignment. The pieces of the task will at this time fall into place. This will probably take at least one class period, but it is time worth spending to insure knowledge of manipulating the software.

4. Assign Task

A student begins an assignment that involves research. As a Media Specialist, I often intervene at this point to see if my assistance in the research process is necessary. It is not uncommon to find that the student not only does not have a clear idea of the assignment, but also is not sure what the outcome—or project—that assesses the assignment will be. That is why, at least for students through Middle School Age, I have students put down their task in writing. In one precise sentence, they should be able to state what the assignment is and how that research will be demonstrated at the outcome of the assignment. For instance: "I will research the Lewis And Clark Expedition and produce a Digital Story which shows what America would be like if this expedition had never occurred." Because the task is written, students will be able to return to the basic assignment from time to time to make sure they are on the right track.

5. Define Expectations

At this point, you have set the stage for the introduction of the assignments to the workgroups. These assignments need to be in the form of essential questions. The students will already be excited about the technology involved with creating a digital story and essential questions will serve to create excitement about the subject matter as well. Give them time to discuss ideas about their topics in their groups and let them dole out assignments of tasks and roles within the groups. It is at this time that you need to define your expectations for the project in the form of a rubric. The rubric should be printed and distributed to each student individually. Each aspect of the rubric needs to be explained and discussed. This part of project is so important that an entire chapter of this book has been devoted to it – Chapter 7. Please review the sample rubrics found there and revise to fit your own needs.

6. Begin Research

This is where the student becomes a seeker and consumer of information. This is where they learn to apply prior knowledge with new knowledge on a particular subject. This is where they investigate the content material, evaluate it, and make decisions as to its relevancy to them objectives. This is where they access information in print, electronically, and through expert resources. This is also where it can all fall to pieces in a matter of minutes. There are some vital organizational aids you need to utilize to help students avoid the pitfalls.

First have each group make a concept map (either diagram on paper or using a program such as Inspiration) to devise a plan to exactly what material they need to find out about. When the map is completed, they can easily divide the research work among group members. The group should check their concept map frequently to add, delete, or modify if necessary. Second, each group needs to begin filling out the BIG6 guide (or other research template, see Chapter 5), which will help them make decisions about the research process. The model is also a constant reminder of the importance of collecting information for use in correctly citing the project. If this research guide is new to your students, you will want to take time to walk them through the process of researching, note-taking, citing information, and synthesizing their research into a digital story.

Most students will tell you they know how to search for information on the Internet. They most likely think that knowing how "to Google" is all there is to the search process. Students who are novices to searching need instruction on Boolean logic techniques, database and subscription sites available, CD-ROM resources, and tips on how to look for biased or inaccurate information. With younger students, I would recommend you give them a list of pre-selected sites where you know they will find good information that is on a level they will understand. Even with my Middle School students, I usually give them lists of web sites I want them to use. This is because with this age of student, no matter what topic they are researching or how good your filtering system at school is, they will end up with rap music lyrics on the screen. It's like magic... only scarier. Anyway, to preserve my sanity and for the sake of time, I give them sites to look up information.

I also do not limit their research to online and electronic sources. This is a great place to teach them how valuable print resources can be, and a perfect place to do "just-in-time" teaching interventions to show them how to effectively use indexes and subject listings to find what they need.

And speaking of teaching interventions, you need to constantly monitor what your students are doing to find those "teachable moments" to guide them in content areas. Remind them to save images and videos on their flash drives that they might want to use later. Help them take notes that are not plagiarized, and show them correct ways to cite their sources.

As individual students collect information and bring it back to the group, they need a folder or notebook to organize information and sources in which they can all have equal access. After a few class periods, the group should have collected enough information to begin the production phase of the assignment.

7. Begin Storyboarding

In the groups, students need to storyboard their information by creating a story on a template provided to them. They need to be reminded that they are telling a story – with a beginning, middle, and end. They need to provide an answer to the essential question they were assigned. They need to place videos and graphic images in the correct sequences. They need to think about the design of their project – components of music, narration, text, and content. Storyboards are rough drafts of the finished product. They do not have to be neat and orderly; in fact, they will probably be revised many times so it might be good to advise students to use pencil. As storyboards are being finalized, students can begin work on narration scripts.

This is also where the group needs to find the right music for their story. Music needs to match the content of the story, in both tempo and mood. In Chapter 4, there are sites that students can use to find copyright-free music to suit their needs.

8. Write Narration

When students need to have voice narration in their story, a script needs to be written down, rehearsed, and pre-recorded using Audacity (Chapter 4). In writing the narration, students need to consider that narrations are usually not wordy or lengthy. Narrations are succinct, clear, and written in the student's own words. Reading from Internet or printed text is not only   uninteresting in a story, it is plagiarism. Depending on how much narration needs to be recorded, this process might be a lengthy one. I encourage students to use a word processing program to write narrations because it can be easily edited and rewritten if necessary. After a good script is written, it can recorded using Audacity and saved to be dropped into the digital story.

9. Produce Product

All the pieces of the puzzle are ready. Images, video clips, music, narration, and storyboard are in place. Students can begin to put the pieces together in the program to make their digital story. Special effects and transitions add to the professional look of the final project. Titles need to be inserted in appropriate places, and the final title screen should contain the citations of the research sources. Special care needs to be taken in checking the spelling on the title frames because it can ruin a great story with only one misspelled word. Digital stories need to be viewed, reviewed, and reviewed again to make sure that all elements are in the correct place and narrations are in the timeline in the proper place. Make sure that a copy of the final project is saved before it is finalized, so if errors are overlooked they can be corrected without beginning the process from square one. When a digital story is in its finalized state—save it often and in many places and many locations. (This is not a book on the "how-to" in using the various programs available to do digital storytelling. There are plenty of other online and print resources available that will aid you in the mechanics of using the software programs (See Chapter 3 for tutorials).

10. Publish & Present Project

When groups present their digital stories, I expect them to do more than click the mouse. I want them to present the story with explanation of how they arrived at their conclusions, engage in some self-reflection on how it turned out. Communication skills such as eye contact, voice, body gestures, poise, and style of presentation are important because they add to the total presentation package of their project. I want them to feel pride in their accomplishment, and I want it to show in their presentation. I share these expectations with them in the form of a rubric that I make available at the beginning of the assignment. This way, they have plenty of time to practice the delivery of their story to the class. These and other rubrics are shared in the next chapter.

11. Assess & 12. Reflect

The last two steps of the process are so important that they actually deserve a chapter devoted to them specifically. Therefore, please continue to Chapter 7 for this information.

Chapter 7

Assessing and Reflecting
On Digital Storytelling Projects

Teacher Assessment

There are two types of tools that need to be utilized in accessing student produced digital stories. The first is the authentic assessment rubrics which students are given at the beginning of the digital storytelling assignment. The rubric will give students a clear understanding of what the teacher's expectations are of the research process, the production process, group dynamics and cooperative learning outcomes, the finished product, and the presentation to the class. Because creating a digital story is a lengthy project, there should be periodic assessments of progress at different stages. The rubric needs to reflect when these periodic assessments will take place and what the teacher will be looking for along the way. Thus, several rubrics need to be created. Every teacher will want to include different things they look for in the project – depending mostly on which type of project they assign. A researched topic digital story rubric will look much different from a creative digital storytelling project rubric.

Sample Rubrics

In recent years, teachers have discovered the simplicity of assessing projects using rubrics, Heidi Goodrich, a rubrics expert, defines a rubric as "a scoring tool that lists the criteria for a piece of work or 'what counts.'" Therefore, a rubric for grading a digital story will the student what the teacher is looking for in the project. Rubrics usually list expectations by quality, i.e., what a Great digital Story looks like all the way down to what a Digital Story looks like that needs more work. Rubrics can help students and teachers define "quality". Rubrics can also help students judge and revise their own work before handing in their assignments.

On the following pages, I have listed examples of rubrics for judging quality of Digital Stories written for different purposes. You can use these examples of rubrics as a springboard to making the rubric that fits your assessment needs.

Content Rubric (Scott County Digital Storytelling Rubric)

Elements	1 – Emerging	2 – Developing	3 – Very Good	4 – Exemplary
1. Evidence of addressing the essential question	Realization is dramatically different than expectation	Realization differs from expectation	Realization from expectation is subtle	Realization and expectation do not differ
2. Point of View Evident	Limited awareness of audience and/or purpose	Some evidence of communication with audience; some lapse in focus	Focuses on purpose; communicates with audience	Establishes a purpose and maintains a clear focus; strong awareness of audience
3. Story has emotional aspect	Audience has little emotional engagement	Audience lapses in emotional engagement	Audience is emotionally engaged	Audience is deeply and emotionally engaged
4. Illustrations, graphics, sound choices match content	Sequential composition; images do not match purpose	Sequential composition; succinct, images & sounds are controlled/logical	Sequential composition; succinct; images & sound create atmosphere and/or tone	Sequential composition; succinct; images & sound creates an atmosphere and/or tone; may communicate symbolism and/or metaphors
5. Pacing of story intrigues audience	Mechanical rhythm; limited use of punctuation; limited vitality	Some rhythm; limited suggestions of emotion via sound effects, lapses in vitality	Engaging rhythm; use of "white space"; evidence of vitality; good use of sound	Engaging rhythm; suggestions of emotions using sound effects; use of "white space"; enhanced vitality

Historical Narrative Rubric (National Standards of US History)

Elements	1 - Emerging	2-Developing	3-Very Good	4-Exemplary
Std 1 Chronological Thinking	Order of events not in sequence	Order of events mostly sequential	Order of events follow sequential order	Order of events sequential and enhanced with flashbacks or other effects
Std 2 Historical Comprehension	Historical narrative does not address purpose; visuals do not illustrate historical events, information inaccurate	Historical narrative somewhat addresses purpose; visuals illustrate historical events; some information inaccurate	Historical narrative addresses purpose; visuals illustrate purpose; information accurate	Historical narrative expands purpose; visuals engage audience with the purpose; information accurate
Std 3 Historical Analysis & Interpretation	Incorrect analysis of cause-and-effect relationships; no relationship of individuals to history; no reference to human role in history	Some cause-and effect relationships noted; individuals relationship to history plays minor role	Cause-and effect relationship evident; importance of human role in history is evident	Cause-and-effect relationships strong; evidence of influence of human role in history, influence of ideas, and the role of chance
Std 5 Historical Research Skills	No evidence of research citations	Incomplete citations of research	Citations of research correctly noted	Citations of research correctly noted; extend bibliography included for further exploration of topic

Cooperative Learning Rubric(Adapted from Participation Rubric Developed by Barbara Frandsen, St. Edward's University

Element	1-Emerging	2-Developing	3-Very Good	4-Exemplary
Work Load	Did less work than the others in group	Did almost as much work as the other in the group	Did an equal amount of work as others in the group	Did a full share of the work – or more than the others in the group
Organization Skills	Did not work with others	Had to be coaxed into doing their part	Worked agreeable with group	Took leadership role in helping group get organized
Creativity	Seemed bored with assignment	Listened to others and made some suggestions	Participate in group discussions	Provided many ideas for project development
Communication	Never expressed excitement and/or frustration	Rarely expressed feeling about assignment	Usually shared feelings and thoughts with group	Clearly communicated ideas, feelings, and thoughts with group
Listening	Refused to accept feedback from group	Argued own point of view over feedback	Reluctantly accepted feedback	Accepted feedback from others willingly
Timeliness	Some work never completed; and other had to complete assignment	Work was usually late but completed in time to be utilized	Work was ready at agreed upon time	Work was ready on time – usually ahead of time

Mechanics Rubric

Elements	1-Emerging	2-Developing	3-Very Good	4-Exemplary
Storyboard	No evidence of storyboard usage	Minimum detail & planning in storyboard format	Good detail & planning of storyboard & digital transitions evident in storyboard	Excellent detail; well planned; effects & transitions evident in storyboard
Audio	Audio is cut-off and inconsistent; Audience has great difficulty hearing narration and soundtrack	Audio not clear in parts; audience understands narration and soundtrack; expression of ideas muddled	Audio is clear; but only partially expresses ideas	Audio is clear; effective communication of ideas; soundtrack enhances story
Editing	No evidence of engaging flow through effects of editing	Scenes have little or no flow; viewer gets lost in story	Most scenes has seamless appearance; good flow and engaging pace	Smooth viewing; seamless appearance; excellent flow
Transitions, Effects	No enhancement of message through effects	Minimal enhancement of message through effects	Somewhat enhances message of the story through effects	Enhances story through effects; completes project
Originality and Creativity	Story shows no originality or creativity	Story shows little originality or creativity	Story show some originality or creativity	Story shows excellent originality and creativity in composition
Documentation	No evidence of citations of sources	Some evidence of citations of sources	Good evidence of citations of sources	Excellent evidence of citations of sources

Peer Assessment

The second type of assessment tool is the peer assessment rubric. This is the tool students will use to judge the quality and effectiveness of other student's projects. The advantage of using this rubric is that when students get feedback from their peers in time to correct deficiencies they often turn in a better and more thoughtful project. Self-correction is an important skill for students to learn and practice.

On the following page is an example of a peer assessment rubric. You will notice that the language in these peer assessments looks much different from the teacher rubric. It has been simplified to make the process less time consuming and yet informative for the group who completed the project being judged.

Peer Review Rubric (Checklist for each category)

Elements	Needs work	Not Bad	Pretty Good	Awesome
I understood the story and could follow your purpose				
I thought the images were chosen carefully and thoughtfully				
I thought the audio was good				
I noticed that you cited all your sources				
I liked your use of effects and transitions				
Overall, this story is rated:				

Reflection

After the presentations are over and grades are given, most teachers have their hands full with planning and implementing the next lesson. Little or no time is allotted to the reflection process on all the aspects of the preceding project. Yet, it is this part of the process that helps us improve our teaching and learning skills and enables us to have insight into how to make similar lessons better, more organized, and avoid many of the pitfalls we fell into this time around. Reflection does not need to be a lengthy or time-consuming process, but will add depth and intensity to your acquired "book of tricks" that we all have as teachers. So, before you close the cover on the digital storytelling lesson, jot down the answers to the following points to use as reference next year, or next semester, or whenever you embark on storytelling again.

- What went right?
- What did the students learn?
- Did higher-level thinking play an important part in the process?
- Did the students learn important multimedia life-skills in the process?
- Was the technology integration seamlessly incorporated into the curriculum?
- What could be improved?
- Did your choice of organization structure work for your students?
- What was outside of your control?
- Did you receive any suggestions from students on how to make the process better? --Maybe you should ask!

Whatever your reflections are, I'll bet you agree with thousands of educators who believe that digital storytelling is a powerful tool for integrating technology into the classroom, accessing the high-level thinking of their students, allowing students to take ownership of their work, and compelling students to engage with content material on a deeper and more personal level. It makes learning fun, activates creativity, and teaches real-world skills which students can use in a variety of circumstances. These intriguing advantages will make digital storytelling increasingly a part of educational practice for many years.

Upon reflection, I have had many "What was I thinking!" moments implementing digital storytelling. So will you. But, if you preserve, you will experience a lot of "Wow!" moments where students show you depths of learning you might never have uncovered using traditional assignments. It makes all the other times worthwhile.

Digital Storytelling

OUT OF the Classroom

Chapter 8

What is Digital Scrapbooking, and is it Different than Digital Storytelling?

I love scrapbooking. Therefore, when the concept of digital storytelling was first introduced to me as a classroom tool to use with my students, I quickly realized the potential of the same process to enhance my scrapbooking hobby. Imagine creating wonderful memories that not only preserve still images for your family forever, but also added the addition of video, sound, music, and special effects and transitions.

Digital scrapbooking is using your computer and special software to create layouts that can be e-mailed or printed out for placement in physical scrapbooks. You can use digital images, scanned photos, clip art, different fonts, and embellishments to create unique and beautiful scrapbook pages without cutting and pasting them into place. It is faster, cleaner, and the results are fantastic! However, digital scrapbooking misses the point as to the wonderful traits in digital storytelling.

Digital storytelling is just as easy to do, but perhaps may take a little longer to complete. Using software that most people already have on their home computers, you can not only preserve the memory of your son's first haircut, but also by adding digital images and video, background music that enhances the story, and your own narration (or maybe even that of your son) that describe the event and keep it as a family treasure forever. Your finished product becomes a CD with such moments saved of all time. You can see the advantages.

Will Digital Storytelling take the place of scrapbooking? Oh no, I will never stop creating my scrapbooks of memories! Now, tucked within the scrapbook page of my son's first haircut are the sights and sounds of that moment that will be there always. Digital storytelling, then, is a fabulous enhancement to the hobby you love. In addition, it engages all the same creative ideas you use in the physical scrapbooking method.

Brief History of Scrapbooking

There is evidence that the concept of using notebooks to preserve information began in the time of Aristotle and Cicero, These men and their students used an early form of our scrapbooking to document their philosophical and religious discussions. During the Renaissance, scholars would copy their favorite passages or poems into blank books to create personal anthologies of works that had inspired or touched them. In the 1800's, Thomas Jefferson would clip newspaper articles about his presidency and save them in a scrapbook. It became vogue during the 1800's for people to place keepsakes such as photos, playbills & ticket stubs along with diaries, locks of children's hair, favorite poems & quotes, and calling cards in albums for safekeeping. The term "scrapbook" came into use during this time when people began using colored paper left over from big printing jobs or "scrap paper" to decorate their keepsake books. Nineteenth century author Mark Twain loved scrapbooking so much that he devoted each Sunday afternoon to his hobby of creating personal scrapbooks. He even patented and sold a series of scrapbooks in the late 1800's. It is said that he made over $50,000 on his scrapbooks.

Through the years, the popularity of scrapbooking has kept pace with a growing population and advances in technology. With the creation of the Internet, scrapbook enthusiasts could communicate online in chat rooms to exchange tips and ideas and hundreds of supply stores came online with supplies for sale. (Slatten, 2004)

Today, with the home computer being commonplace in American homes, software programs for scrapbooking have added dimension to this tradition of preserving memories. And, with the addition of video and audio, the scrapbooking has become completely digital and instead of saving keepsakes in an album, they are safeguarded on CD or DVD.

No matter how scrapbooking is accomplished, the concept remains the same. We have just moved on to utilize the cutting-edge methods we now have access to, which only serves to enhance our creative energy to create more innovative finished products. The technology we have available to us today will probably also seem old-fashioned someday as technology continues to find new ways to improve how we do work.

Can you do it? Of course you can. This part of the book will guide you in this endeavor. Chapter 9 will give you the basics of the process, and instruction from beginning to end of how to use this new technique of digital storytelling. Chapter 10 will provide resources you will want to use, and helpful Internet resources to enhance your projects. Ready? Let's go!

Chapter 9

Tools for Digital
Scrapbooking/Storytelling

W̶e will be looking at two types of digital scrapbooks. The first is creating digital pages that look similar to the physical pages you create with paper and glue. You create the page using templates that you can create or buy and add your own digital photos, embellishments, designs, fonts, and text. You can then save the completed page to a file on your computer. After you have collected a series of completed pages, you can drop them into a program such as PhotoStory3 (Windows) and add narration, soundtrack, and elements of movement, special effects, and transitions. The finished digital album can be saved on your computer, saved on CD or DVD, e-mail to a friend or relative, or added to an individual webpage.

The second type of digital scrapbook uses programs that allow you combine digital photos (from digital cameras or physical photos that have been digitized using a scanner) with video (from camcorders or clips taken from online sources) and add enhancements such as voice narration, music, and effects and transitions. The finished product is a computer file "album" which captures both audio and visual memories and can be imported to e-mail, web pages, or saved to CD or DVD.

Both of the methods are easy to learn. Both give incredibly satisfying creative experiences for the scrapbooker and result in wonderful products to share with others. We will talk about each method and how they can be used.

Method 1: Digital Photo Album

If you have never used digital templates to design scrapbook pages, then you need to download some sample pages and practice with them. Here are some sites where you can find sample downloads of digital scrapbook templates:

- **Cottage Arts**
  http://www.cottagearts.net/samples.html

  Nine different sets of digital pages and embellishments for different themes will give you a fell for working with your digital image editor.

- **Birthday Scrapbook Page Layouts**
  http://scrapbooking.about.com/od/layouts/ig/Birthday-Scrapbook-Page-Ideas/index.htm

  At this site, you can see how some finished products look before they are dropped into a program to provide audio and effects.

- **DC Designs**
  http://daleanncubbagedesigns.blogspot.com/

  A site featuring Storyboard Templates, Page Templates, Greeting Card Templates, Birth Announcement Templates, and MORE

Next, you need software. Here are some choices:

Program	Learning Curve	Time	Cost	Flexibility
Adobe Photoshop	High	High	High	High
Adobe Photoshop Elements	Medium	Medium	Low	High
JASC Paint Shop Pro	Medium	Medium	Medium	High
Ulead PhotoImpact	Medium	Medium	Medium	High
Microsoft Digital Image Pro	Low	Low	Medium	Medium
Corel Draw	High	High	High	High
FotoFusion	Low	Low	Low	Low
CK Scrapbook Designer	Low	Low	Low	Low
HP Scrapbook Assistant	Low	Low	Low	Low
RXFoto Creative	Low	Low	Low	Medium

I use Photoshop but you can use whatever photo editor you have or can afford. Import the background paper into the editor first and save it under a filename of your choice. Then add photos and resize them to your liking and drag them to a location you choose. TIP: once you add photos to the template, you may want to rename the file to you can easily backup to make changes if necessary. Save every time you add an element from this point. If the template you are using contains picture frames, you will want to move the photo to the back of the frame. If the template package sample you are using contains embellishments, you may want to add some to the page. Using the tools of your photo-editing program, you can add a title using the font, color and size of your choice. If you need to add other text on the page, use the text box to do so. Remember, if you are going to put the finished page in a PhotoStory3 album, you will have the opportunity to narrate the page. You will not want many words to distract your audience if you plan to use narration and music.

The final effect you might want to use is drop shadows to dramatize parts of your page. After you have your page to your satisfaction, you can print it, resize it, or save it. Save it as a .jpg so you can import it into the PhotoStory3 program later. The .jpg format is also a smaller file to use if you are planning to e-mail the page to anyone.

After you have collected several pages, you can practice you digital storytelling using PhotoStory3 (Windows). PhotoStory3 is a program that runs on the XP operating system and is available as a free download at:

http://www.microsoft.com/windowsxp/using/digitalphotography/photostory/default.mspx .

Import your pages into the program and drag-and-drop them in the order you want. Now you need to find the music that will best go with your theme. In the next chapter are resources of non-copyrighted music you can download, then import into PhotoStory3, then drop into the music track.

If you need narration for your story, my suggestion is that you use a free download program called audacity to record your narrative. Audacity can be downloaded from http://audacity.sourceforge.net/. To have the most professional results while recording using audacity, you will want to use a headset/microphone combo unit that plugs into your computer. These units are inexpensive and available at computer stores everywhere. Once you have recorded, save the recording, import it into your PhotoStory3 program and drop it into the narration track where it best fits. You will want to record the narrative for each page in your story separately so you can manipulate them to fit the pages.

At this point, you can add titles; insert text frames, and add credits at the end. Use the special effects to zoom in and out of pages to give the impression of movement. Use the transitions to move from page to page. The page-turner transition is the one I like to use for scrapbooking albums.

When you have previewed your story, and are satisfied with the results, save a copy of the project before you finalize it. This way, you can easily go back and re-edit if necessary. The final step is to finalize your project. Save it on your computer, insert it into web pages, or burn it to CD or DVD to keep with your paper version of scrapbook as an enhancement. And that's it. You have created a digital photo album.

I have listed many sources of other templates that you can buy and download. They are all beautiful, creatively made, and easy to use. If you are very artistic and have the time, you can use a Paint program to create your own templates. Either way, digital photo albums are great keepsakes for your family.

Digital Story Scrapbooks

      The difference between the digital photo album and the digital scrapbook is the addition of video to your scrapbook. Using MovieMake2 (Windows) or iMovie (MAC), you can create magical keepsakes. First, you need to look for the program on your computer. MovieMaker2 requires XP operating system. After you open the program, you can import video clips you have filmed using your camcorder, or video clips you have found on the Internet. Then, import digital photos, or pages you have made using templates as described in the procedure above. Import the music of your choice, and narration made using Audacity (see procedure above). In a procedure similar to PhotoStory3, drag-and drop various elements of your story, add effects and transitions, preview, and save. Samples of digital stories that you can look at to get ideas for your own creation can be found in Chapter 10.

Chapter 10

Resources for Digital Story Scrapbooks

Digital Scrapbook Templates

Scrapbook Max

Comes with everything you need to make your own digital scrapbooks. Start with a ready-to-use scrapbook theme - then add your own photos, captions and text. It's as easy as pointing and clicking with your mouse.

http://www.scrapbookmax.com/site/index.php?gad=CNjD9LOCEgip8iXXT ZndPRju2cD_AyC8ksgP

SimplyReady Digital Scrapbooking

SimplyReady Digital Scrapbooking software includes a photo editor that allows you to crop, stretch, rotate, and flip photos so they fit perfectly. With so many backgrounds and embellishments included, you'll have everything you need to create hundreds of original, eye-catching scrapbook pages with your digital photos.

http://www.simplyreadyscrapbooking.com/affiliate.asp

Computer Scrapbook.com

Digital Scrapbooking Element Kits are intricate digital designs for use in design applications like Adobe PhotoShop, Paint Shop Pro, and Picture It!

http://www.computerscrapbook.com/elements.html

Digital Scrapbook Ideas

Scrapbook.com

At this site find many finished digital pages to give you ideas for your own creations. Also look for poems, quotes, and articles to inspire great scrapbook pages.

http://www.scrapbook.com/

Digital Scrapbooking Tools

FotoFinish software

FotoFinish SUITE is the easy photo scrapbooking software that allows you to create great-looking photo scrapbook pages in a snap! Download a free 30-day trail version at the website below. It sells for about $99.

http://www.fotofinish.com/specials/photo-scrapbook.asp?id=41476

How to retouch and/or "clone" images

Joanne Perry, from Pennsylvania, shares these tips for editing digital photos.

http://www.discoveryeducatornetwork.com/objects/content_revision/download.cfm/revision_id.203819/workspace_id.124855/Cloning%20and%20Retouching%20digital%20photos.doc/

Microsoft PhotoStory

This program allows you to organize digital pictures, narrate them, organize them, add a soundtrack (your music or from the software), and create a *.wmv movie file that can play in Windows Media Player.

Windows MovieMaker

This program allows you to import digital video from your camcorder using a USB cable, edit the video, and add narration and music. You can also import Internet video clips. This program produces a professional looking video in *.wmv format that can play in Windows Media Player.

Both software applications require an up-to-date version of Windows Media Player, available from Microsoft as a free download.

Windows MovieMaker Download:

http://www.microsoft.com/windowsxp/downloads/updates/moviemaker2.mspx

Windows MovieMaker Tutorials:

http://www.microsoft.com/windowsxp/using/moviemaker/default.mspx

http://www.microsoft.com/windowsxp/using/moviemaker/getstarted/default.mspx

http://www.mightycoach.com/articles/mm2/index.html

http://www.mightycoach.com/articles/mm2/savingprojects-moviemaker2.html

http://www.ita.sel.sony.com/support/tutorials/usb-streaming/

http://www.fluffbucket.com/othettutorials/video/wmmaker.htm

http://www.atomiclearning.com/moviemaker2

http://www.windowsmoviemakers.net/Tutorials/HowToMovieMaker.aspx

http://core.ecu.edu/vel/itc/tutorials/moviemaker.html

http://www.eicsoftware.com/PapaJohn/MM2/PS3-Intro.html

http://www.bobsedulinks.com/digital.htm

Microsoft PhotoStory Download:

http://www.microsoft.com/windowsxp/using/digitalphotography/photostory/default.mspx

Microsoft PhotoStory Tutorials:

http://www.eicsoftware.com/PapaJohn/MM2/PS3-Intro.html

http://www.eicsoftware.com/PapaJohn/MM2/MM2.html

http://www.bobsedulinks.com/digital.htm

http://www.microsoft.com/windowsxp/using/digitalphotography/photostory/tips/create.mspx

http://msmvps.com/chrisl/archive/2004/10/27/16816.aspx

http://www.windowsphotostory.com/

http://graphicssoft.about.com/b/a/122245.htm

Windows Media Player 10 Download:

http://www.microsoft.com/downloads/details.aspx?FamilyID=b446ae53-3759-40cf-80d5-cde4bbe07999&displaylang=en

Flickr and Bubblr

Flickr is an online site that allows you to store, search, sort and share digital photos. Bubblr is its companion site that allows you to make comic strips using your digital photos by adding word balloons and thought balloons to them. And, it is a free resource.

Flickr: http://www.flickr.com/

Bubblr: http://www.pimpampum.net/bubblr/

Scrapbooking has entered a new and exciting arena that will exploit your creativity and ingenuity. The results are surprisingly professional and satisfying. It is the smart new way to tell your personal digital stories.

Chapter 11

Putting It All Together

A Word about Copyright

The Education Use Exemption (Section 107 of the Copyright Act) does apply to digital storytelling. To use this exemption, certain guidelines must be followed. In order to determined whether a certain use is considered fair, the statute directs that the following factors be considered:

- Purpose and character of use
- Nature of the work in question
- Amount of work that is used
- Effect on the potential market for the work

There are similar guidelines applied to the educational use of music, and streaming audio and digital content. Short copyrighted digital video clips used in production of student digital stories is most likely considered fair use; however, use of an entire video would be considered a violation. Use of digital video in the public domain is always legal. It is always best to ask permission when dealing with any copyrighted material however, and this can be accomplished by contacting the Copyright Clearance Commission. Most of the time, permission will be granted for educational purposes for a limited time of use. (http://www.copyright.com)

Teachers need to be especially aware that there is a huge difference between using copyrighted material in the classroom and posting student projects using copyrighted material to the Internet. If you intend to publish student projects or enter them into any of the growing number of competitions of digital stories, then you must be especially concerned that all permissions have been granted and citations listed correctly. We do not want to stifle any student creativity, but we, as educators, must be the watchdogs of copyright infractions to avoid any conflict down the road.

The following Internet sites will help you determine the ins and outs of Copyright and the TEACH Act for Educational Fair Use:

Copyright Primer: http://www-apps.umuc.edu/primer/enter.php

Digital Copyright Primer: http://www-apps.umuc.edu/dcprimer/enter.php

Finishing Touches

No matter how you use Digital Storytelling – in the classroom or out of the classroom, you will find it to be intriguing. It has the power to unleash individual creativity that results in surprisingly professional quality results. It is a satisfying experience and one in which I hope you will continue to enjoy with your students and for yourself for many years to come.

BIBLIOGRAPHY

Eisenberg, Michael B. and Doug Johnson. <u>Computer Skills for Information Problem-Solving: Learning and Teaching Technology in Context</u>. Syracuse, NY: ERIC Clearinghouse on Information and Technology, 1996.

<u>http://www.creatingthe21stcentury.org/Intro6-bebefits-story.html</u> John Seely, Brown, Steve Denning, Katalina Groh, Larry Prusak. <u>Storytelling: Passport to the 21st Century. </u> Accessed: August 3, 2006.

<u>http://www.digitales.us/story_details.php?story_id=12</u> Students of Brooks Magnet School, Wichita, KS. <u>Grass Born to be Stepped On</u> Accessed: August 7, 2006.

<u>http://www.pagesoftheheart.net/artman/publish/article_727.shtml</u> LeeAndra G. Slatten. <u>A Brief History of Scrapbooking. Accessed: August 20, 2006.</u>

<u>http://www.sscnet.ucla.edu/nchs/standards/thinking5-12.html</u> National Center for History in the Schools. Accessed: August 19, 2006.

<u>http://www.stedwards.edu/cte/resources/grub.htm</u> Dr. Barbara Frandsen. Cooperative Learning Rubric. Accessed August 19, 2006.

Pellowski, Anne. <u>The World of Storytelling. </u> New York, R.R. Bowker, 1977.

Printed in the United States
70643LV00004B/295-297